First Print Edition [1.0] -1440 h. (2019 c.e.)

Copyright © 1440 H./2019 C.E.
Taalib al-Ilm Educational Resources

http://taalib.com
Learn Islaam, Live Islaam.^{SM}

ISBN EAN-13:   978-1-938117-64-0   [Soft cover Print Edition]

From the Publisher

GOLDEN WORDS UPON GOLDEN WORDS…FOR EVERY MUSLIM.

"Imaam al-Barbahaaree, may Allaah have mercy upon him said:

May Allaah have mercy upon you! Examine carefully the speech of everyone you hear from in your time particularly. So do not act in haste and do not enter into anything from it until you ask and see: Did any of the Companions of the Prophet, may Allaah's praise and salutations be upon him, speak about it, or did any of the scholars? So if you find a narration from them about it, cling to it, do not go beyond it for anything and do not give precedence to anything over it and thus fall into the Fire.

Explanation by Sheikh Saaleh al-Fauzaan, may Allaah preserve him:

'Do not be hasty in accepting as correct what you may hear from the people, especially in these later times. As now there are many who speak about so many various matters, issuing rulings and ascribing to themselves both knowledge and the right to speak. This is especially the case after the emergence and spread of new modern day media technologies. Such that everyone now can speak and bring forth that which is, in truth, worthless; by this, meaning words of no true value - speaking about whatever they wish in the name of knowledge and in the name of the religion of Islaam. It has even reached the point that you find the people of misguidance and the members of the various groups of misguidance and deviance from the religion speaking as well. Such individuals have now become those who speak in the name of the religion of Islaam through means such as the various satellite television channels. Therefore be very cautious!

It is upon you, oh Muslim, and upon you, oh student of knowledge, individually, to verify matters and not rush to embrace everything and anything you may hear. It is upon you to verify the truth of what you hear, asking, 'Who else also makes this same statement or claim?', 'Where did this thought or concept originate or come from?', 'Who is its reference or source authority?' Asking what are the evidences which support it from within the Book and the Sunnah? And inquiring where has the individual who is putting this forth studied and taken his knowledge from? From who has he studied the knowledge of Islaam?

Each of these matters requires verification through inquiry and investigation, especially in the present age and time. It is not every speaker who should rightly be considered a source of knowledge, even if he is well spoken and eloquent and can manipulate words captivating his listeners. Do not be taken in and accept him until you are aware of the degree and scope of what he possesses of knowledge and understanding. Perhaps someone's words may be few, but possess true understanding, and perhaps another will have a great deal of speech yet he is actually ignorant to such a degree that he doesn't actually possess anything of true understanding. Rather he only has the ability to enchant with his speech so that the people are deceived. Yet he puts forth the perception that he is a scholar, that he is someone of true understanding and comprehension, that he is a capable thinker, and so forth. Through such means and ways he is able to deceive and beguile the people, taking them away from the way of truth.

Therefore, what is to be given true consideration is not the amount of the speech put forth or that one can extensively discuss a subject. Rather, the criterion that is to be given consideration is what that speech contains within it of sound authentic knowledge, what it contains of the established and transmitted principles of Islaam. Perhaps a short or brief statement which is connected to or has a foundation in the established principles can be of greater benefit than a great deal of speech which simply rambles on, and through hearing you don't actually receive very much benefit from.

This is the reality which is present in our time; one sees a tremendous amount of speech which only possesses within it a small amount of actual knowledge. We see the presence of many speakers, yet few people of true understanding and comprehension.' "

[The eminent major scholar Sheikh Saaleh al-Fauzaan, may Allaah preserve him- 'A Valued Gift for the Reader Of Comments Upon the Book Sharh as-Sunnah', page 102-103]

Is not He better than your so-called gods, He Who originates creation and shall then repeat it, and Who provides for you from heaven and earth? Is there any god with Allaah? Say: 'Bring forth your proofs, if you are truthful.' -(Surah an-Naml: 64)

Explanation: *Say: "Bring forth your proofs.."* This is a command for the Prophet, may Allaah's praise and salutation be upon him, to rebuke them immediately after they had put forward their own rebuke. Meaning: '*Say to them: bring your proof, whether it is an intellectual proof or a proof from transmitted knowledge, that would stand as evidence that there is another with Allaah, the Most Glorified and the Most Exalted*'. Additionally, it has been said that it means: '*Bring your proof that there is anyone other than Allaah, the Most High, who is capable of doing that which has been mentioned from His actions, the Most Glorified and the Most Exalted.*' *...if you are truthful.* meaning, in this claim. From this it is derived that a claim is not accepted unless clearly indicated by evidences."

[Tafseer al-'Aloosee: vol. 15, page 14]

Sheikh Rabee'a Ibn Hadee Umair al-Madkhalee, may Allaah preserve him said,

'It is possible for someone to simply say, "*So and so said such and such.*" However we should say, "*Produce your proof.*" So why did you not ask them for their proof by saying to them: "*Where was this said?*" Ask them questions such as this, as from your weapons are such questions as: "*Where is this from? From which book? From which cassette?...*" '

[The Overwhelming Falsehoods of 'Abdul-Lateef Bashmeel' page 14]

The guiding scholar Imaam Sheikh 'Abdul-'Azeez Ibn Abdullah Ibn Baaz, may Allaah have mercy upon him, said,

'It is not proper that any intelligent individual be misled or deceived by the great numbers from among people from the various countries who engage in such a practice. As the truth is not determined by the numerous people who engage in a matter, rather the truth is known by the Sharee'ah evidences. Just as Allaah the Most High says in Surah al-Baqarah, *And they say, "None shall enter Paradise unless he be a Jew or a Christian." These are only their own desires. Say "Produce your proof if you are truthful."* -(Surah al-Baqarah: 111) And Allaah the Most High says *And if you obey most of those on the earth, they will mislead you far away from Allaah's path. They follow nothing but conjectures, and they do nothing but lie.* -(Surah al-'Ana'an: 116)'

[Collection of Rulings and Various Statements of Sheikh Ibn Baaz -Vol. 1 page 85]

Sheikh Muhammad Ibn 'Abdul-Wahaab, may Allaah have mercy upon him, said,

'Additionally, verify that knowledge held regarding your beliefs, distinguishing between what is correct and false within it, coming to understand the various areas of knowledge of faith in Allaah alone and the required disbelief in all other objects of worship. You will certainly see various different matters which are called towards and enjoined; so if you see that a matter is in fact one coming from Allaah and His Messenger, then this is what is intended and is desired that you possess. Otherwise, Allaah has certainly given you that which enables you to distinguish between truth and falsehood, if Allaah so wills.

Moreover, this writing of mine- do not conceal it from the author of that work; rather present it to him. He may repent and affirm its truthfulness and then return to the guidance of Allaah, or perhaps if he says that he has a proof for his claims, even if that is only a single statement, or if he claims that within my statements there is something unsupported, then request his evidence for that assertion. After this if there is something which continues to cause uncertainty or is a problem for you, then refer it back to me, so that then you are aware of both his statement and mine in that issue. We ask Allaah to guide us, you, and all the Muslims to that which He loves and is pleased with.'

[Personal Letters of Sheikh Muhammad Ibn 'Abdul-Wahaab- Conclusion to Letter 20]

Sheikh 'Abdullah Ibn 'Abdur-Rahman Abu Bateen, may Allaah have mercy upon him, said,

'And for an individual, if it becomes clear to him that something is the truth, he should not turn away from it and or be discouraged simply due to the few people who agree with him and the many who oppose him in that, especially in these latter days of this present age.

If the ignorant one says: "*If this was the truth so and so and so and so would have been aware of it!*" However this is the very claim of the disbelievers, in their statement found in the Qur'aan ❨ *If it had truly been good, they would not have preceded us to it!* ❩-(Surah al-Ahqaaf: 11) and in their statement ❨ *Is it these whom Allaah has favored from amongst us?* ❩-(Surah al-Ana'am: 53). Yet certainly, as Alee Ibn Abee Taalib, may Allaah be pleased with him, stated "*Know the truth and then you will know it' people.*" But for the one who generally stands upon confusion and uncertainty, then every doubt swirls around him. And if the majority of the people were in fact upon the truth today, then Islaam would not be considered strange, yet, by Allaah, it is today seen as the most strange of affairs!"

[Durar As-Sanneeyyah -vol. 10, page 400]

Foundations For The New Muslim & Newly Striving Muslim

A Journey through Selected Questions & Answers
with Sheikh 'Abdul-'Azeez Ibn 'Abdullah Ibn Baaz

[Exercise Workbook]

Compiled and Translated by:
Abu Sukhailah Khalil Ibn-Abelahyi

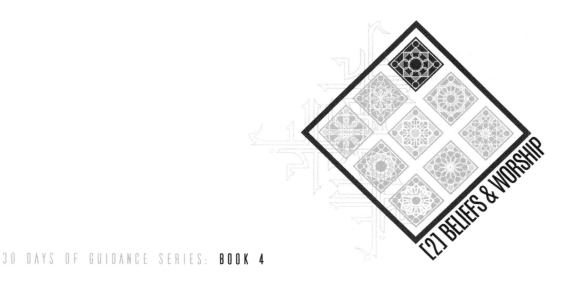

How to use this Exercise Workbook

This workbook can be used to make it simpler for the one administering a study circle to check all exercise homework from the answer key which is available at the back of the [Self-Study / Teachers Edition].The exercise workbooks can be collected after class or at another convenient time for student work to be checked before proceeding to the next day.

A small marking area has been added for indicating correct and incorrect answers at the bottom of each page. Depending on question type , there is a [/ 4] or [/ 8] for recording the number of correct answers out of total answers on that specific page. Partial scores can be given for essay answers that may not completely fulfill the needed answer, and then clarifying notes added in the teacher notes section below the same essay answer area..

SCORING EACH DAYS EXERCISE ASSESSMENT TOTAL

Multiply the total points of correct answers for each day or lesson (max. 8) times (X) 12.5 for score out of 100.

Individual instructors or teachers can choose to score the single comprehensive understanding question for extra credit at their discretion. However this single discussion question is not included or scored in the individual online assessments on the website.

In explaining the meaning of a narration from Hudhaifah, may Allaah be pleased with him, who said:

"Oh group of al-qurraa'! Be steadfast, for if you do so you will be those who have significantly excelled in what is correct. But if you diverge towards the right or left, then you will go astray, far astray." [1]

Sheikh Ibn Baaz, may Allaah have mercy upon him, states,
"The meaning of *'be steadfast'* is to be steadfast upon the straight path. And what is meant by *'al-qurraa''* is those who are scholars and seekers of knowledge. As such is means, 'be steadfast upon the path of religion of Allaah'. As if a worshipper is steadfast in Islaam, then he excels forward in what is correct significantly. However, if a worshiper diverges to the right or to the left, towards the paths of misguidance, then he goes astray, far astray.

As such it is an obligation to hold firmly to undertaking whatever Allaah has legislated, and be far away from everything Allaah is displeased with, as Allah says, ❴*Or have they partners with Allaah – false gods who have instituted for them a religion which Allaah has not ordained?*❵- (Surah ash-Shura: 21) Proceed upon the straight path, even if with limited good deeds. As proceeding along with the obedient worshippers doing limited deeds, is better that to proceeding upon any of the various paths or ways which have deviated away from the way of truth. As even if someone is doing injustice to himself through falling into some sins and transgressions, he is still proceeding upon the path of ultimate success.

But as for someone who proceeds upon any way other than Islaam, or who desires to bring into Islaam the false practices of the period before the coming of Islaam to humanity, this individual walks upon the path of someone destroying and ruining himself. So we ask Allaah for safety and well being."

(From 'Comments of Sheikh Ibn Baaz Upon the Book the Merits of Islaam by Sheikh Muhammad Ibn 'Abdul-Wahaab', pg 11)

---

[1]   Saheeh al-Bukharee, no 7282

TABLE OF CONTENTS

THE "30 DAYS OF GUIDANCE" SERIES

The goal of the "*30 Days of Guidance*" book series is to better enable us, as worshipers of Allaah, to embody and reflect in the various different areas of life for a Muslim, our connection and adherence to the believer's path of the first three believing generations. Many Muslims, due to lacking opportunities to study consistently and be cultivated at the feet of noble steadfast scholars, have an inconsistency they themselves recognize- an inconsistency between the clear path of Islaam of the first Muslims, which they have connected themselves to, and what they have actually been successful in making a daily reality in their practice of Islaam. Sheikh Saaleh Ibn al-Fauzaan, may Allaah preserve him, explained the importance of striving to rectify this,

*"... For the one who proceeds upon the methodology of the best generations, even if that is during the very last days of the existence of earth, then he is safe, saved, and protected from entering the Hellfire. As Allaah, the Most Glorified and the Most Exalted, said, ❦**And the first to embrace Islaam of the Muhaajiroon (those who migrated from Makkah to Al-Madinah) and the Ansaar (the citizens of Al-Madinah who helped and gave aid to the Muhaajiroon) and also those who followed them exactly (in faith). Allaah is well-pleased with them as they are well-pleased with Him. He has prepared for them Gardens under which rivers flow (Paradise), to dwell therein forever. That is the supreme success.**❧—*(Surah Al-Tawbah:100)*

*So Allaah, the Most Exalted, the Most Magnificent, has included and described them as those who follow Muhaajiroon and the Ansaar, upon a condition, "**who followed them exactly (in faith).**" Meaning truly followed them with precision and integrity, not merely putting forth a claim or outwardly attributing or attaching themselves to them without actually realizing their guidance. This is true whether that shortfall is caused by ignorance or by the following of desires. Not everyone who attributes himself to the first three generations is true in his assertion unless he follows them precisely and with integrity. This is in fact a condition, a condition placed by Allaah, the Most Glorified and the Most Exalted. The wording "**exactly (in faith).** meaning precisely, with integrity, as well as entirely.*

What is required in truly following them is that you study the methodology of the Salaf, that you understand it, and that you are firmly attached to it. But as for individuals who simply attribute themselves to them, while they do not really understand their methodology nor their way, then this does not really benefit them with anything, and does not actually help them in any way. Such people are not from those upon the way of the Salaf and should not be considered Salafees, because they are not following the first generations precisely with integrity, as indeed Allaah, the Most Glorified and the Most Exalted, has placed this as the condition for their following of them to be true.

....The one who proceeds upon the methodology of the Salaf must have two characteristics, as we have previously mentioned. Firstly, actually understanding the methodology of the first generations, and the second matter is adhering firmly to it, even when it causes him hardship and discomfort. As he will certainly encounter a great deal of that from those who oppose this path of guidance. He will encounter harassment. He will encounter stubbornness. He will encounter false accusations. He will face having directed towards him evil names and false labels. However, he must remain patient in the face of this, as he is convinced and satisfied with what he stands upon. He should be not shaken or troubled in the face of a whirlwind of difficulties. He should not be affected or changed by what he encounters of different trials, but remains patient when facing them until he meets his Lord.

Accordingly, one must firstly learn the methodology of the first three generations, and then follow it exactly with integrity, while being patient with what he encounters from the people due to this adherence. Yet this, in and of itself, is also not enough; it is additionally necessary to spread the methodology of the first generations. It is required to invite the people to Allaah and invite them to the way of the Salaf, to explain it to the people and spread this way among them. The one who does this is Salafee in reality and truth. But as for the one who claims Salafeeyah, yet he does not truly understand the methodology of the Salaf, or he does indeed understand it yet fails to truly follow it, but simply follows what the people are upon, or merely follows what happens to agree with his desires, this one is not Salafee, even if he calls and labels himself that.

This fact demands from us that we place great importance in fully comprehending the way of the first generations and studying their methodology in beliefs, character, and actions in every environment and situation. As the path and methodology of the first three generations is that methodology upon which the Messenger of Allaah, may the praise and salutations be upon him, was upon, and is that way which those who follow the best of generations and walk upon their path, will proceed upon until the Final Hour is established....

...As such, it is required that the one who claims this way, or connects himself to the Salaf make this descriptive name a reality and make his attachment to them something which truly reflects the way of the first generations in beliefs, and in statements, and in actions, and in general dealings so that he may be a true Salafee and that he may be a righteous example to others and someone who sincerely reflects the way of the righteous first generations of Islaam.” [1]

We ask Allaah for success in each of our efforts to both learn and reflect the clear path of the first three generations, in every area of our individual lives, the lives of our spouses, and the lives of our children. And the success is from Allaah.

---

[1]   From the lecture “Salafeeyah, Its Reality And Its Characteristics” http://www.alfawzan.af.org.sa/

DAY 1: HOW DO WE KNOW THAT OUR ISLAAM IS CORRECT?

TEST YOUR UNDERSTANDING:

TRUE & FALSE QUESTIONS

[Chose true or false for each individual sentence from today's content.]

4 min

01. Sincerity is beneficial but not required for becoming Muslim.   [T / F]

02. None of our deeds are accepted without sincerity.   [T / F]

03. Every Muslim must believe that Muhammad was sent to all of the worlds.   [T / F]

04. Whatever we feel should be part of our Islaam we can accept and practice.   [T / F]

FILL IN THE BLANK QUESTIONS

[Enter the correct individual word to complete the sentences from today's content.]

8 min

05. Someone should embrace Islaam seeking the _____ of Allaah.

06. A _____ does things outwardly, but without inwardly believing in them.

07. All of our actions should conform to the _____ guidelines.

08. Allaah said about Islaam, ❨*...so follow it and do not follow the* _____ *of those who do not know.*❩

INTERACTIVE DISCUSSION QUESTION

COMPREHENSIVE UNDERSTANDING QUESTION

3-7 min

[*]. Discuss any major challenge someone faces when embracing Islaam, what are possible ways to face that difficulty?

TEACHER NOTES / CORRECTIONS

✳[/ *]

TEST YOUR UNDERSTANDING:

4 min

TRUE & FALSE QUESTIONS

[Chose true or false for each individual sentence from today's content.]

01. In the future Islaam will now never be seen as strange, as it is a [T / F]
major religion.

02. Peoples' understanding of the Sunnah can be corrupted. [T / F]

03. There will always be a large number of righteous Muslims. [T / F]

04. When the Muslims first moved to Medina they were not longer [T / F]
strangers.

8 min

FILL IN THE BLANK QUESTIONS

[Enter the correct individual word to complete the sentences from today's content.]

05. Islaam originally began with only a few people who were considered
strange in the city of _____.

06. The strangers may be those who have _____ from their families
and tribes due to following Islaam.

07. The strangers may be a _____ righteous people following Islaam
amongst many people practicing wrongdoing and disobedience

08. The strangers, due to following Islaam, remain _____ upon the
obedience of Allaah and truly following his religion.

3-7min

COMPREHENSIVE UNDERSTANDING QUESTION

[*]. What is one possible aspect of why general people consider or see Islaam as something strange today?

TEACHER NOTES / CORRECTIONS

✳[/ *]

TEST YOUR UNDERSTANDING:

4 min

TRUE & FALSE QUESTIONS

[Chose true or false for each individual sentence from today's content.]

01. It is enough that a Muslim believes in and thanks Allaah in their heart. [T / F]

02. A Muslim must believe in everything authentic transmitted from the Messenger of Allaah. [T / F]

03. The first thing a new Muslim must do is perform the five pillars of Islaam [T / F]

04. A person who only neglects some of the pillars of Islaam still has strong faith. [T / F]

8 min

FILL IN THE BLANK QUESTIONS

[Enter the correct individual word to complete the sentences from today's content.]

05. It is affirmed that emaan or faith in Allaah of the worshippers both increases and _____.

06. It is _____ that a Muslim engages in the ritual prayer as well as the other obligatory matters.

07. The Prophet, said, *{That which _____ us from the disbelievers is our performance of salaat. He who abandons it, becomes a disbeliever.}*

08. The neglecting to perform salaat it is considered major _____ among many of the scholars.

COMPREHENSIVE UNDERSTANDING QUESTION

3-7 min

[*]. Give examples of three acts of worship from the Sunnah that clearly have a required inner aspect as well as a required outer aspect.

TEACHER NOTES / CORRECTIONS

[/]

TEST YOUR UNDERSTANDING:

4 min

TRUE & FALSE QUESTIONS

[Chose true or false for each individual sentence from today's content.]

01. An individual becomes Muslim by stating the two testimonies [T / F] of faith.

02. If someone mocks the religion of Islaam, it takes them outside [T / F] of the religion.

03. We can accept and choose those aspects of Islaam which like. [T / F]

04. The Companions did not hold that neglecting actions affected [T / F] ones' Islaam.

8 min

FILL IN THE BLANK QUESTIONS

[Enter the correct individual word to complete the sentences from today's content.]

05. If someone enters into Islaam by _____ stating the two testimonies of faith, then at that point we judge them as someone within Islaam.

06. If someone who says they are Muslim, rejects the obligation of the ritual prayer, they become someone who has _____ the religion.

07. If someone who says they are Muslim _____ the religion of Islaam, or curses Allaah or curses the Messenger, they become someone who has left the religion.

08. By denying the general _____ fasting of Ramadhaan, a person negates their Islaam by this denial or disavowing.

COMPREHENSIVE UNDERSTANDING QUESTION

3-7min

[*].   What is the difference between someone who denies something from Islaam out of ignorance, and someone who knowingly rejects an obligatory part of Islaam?

TEACHER NOTES / CORRECTIONS

✻[/ *]

TEST YOUR UNDERSTANDING:

4 min

TRUE & FALSE QUESTIONS

[Chose true or false for each individual sentence from today's content.]

01. We can perform the Hajj in any way that feels correct to us, as it is symbolic. [T / F]

02. If a Muslim was neglectful of learning before doing something then asking afterwards does not benefit them. [T / F]

03. We should consider authentic knowledge part of preparing for our acts of worship. [T / F]

04. We should ask about matters of worship beforehand, but if we forget then we can proceed as we see fit. [T / F]

8 min

FILL IN THE BLANK QUESTIONS

[Enter the correct individual word to complete the sentences from today's content.]

05. What is required upon a Muslim is that they ask someone of knowledge _____ they begin engaging in acts of worship.

06. A Muslim should take the initiative to ask before undertaking the various forms of ritual _____.

07. It is important is that a Muslim learns and gains _____ about aspects of his religion.

08. If a Muslim makes mistakes in his ritual worship, seeking knowledge of those specific matters becomes _____ upon them individually.

COMPREHENSIVE UNDERSTANDING QUESTION

3-7min

DAY - 05

[*]. Discuss a possible example of how a failure to seek knowledge and ask about the guidance of Islaam in a religious matter in our lives can have serious consequences.

TEACHER NOTES / CORRECTIONS

✳[/ *]

TEST YOUR UNDERSTANDING:

4 min

TRUE & FALSE QUESTIONS

[Chose true or false for each individual sentence from today's content.]

01. A person is not free to chose their path in life but must simply [T / F] follow what is decreed for them.

02. Our free will and choices mean that Allaah cannot decree [T / F] anything absolutely.

03. Allaah's decree sets up limits and boundaries that we can act [T / F] independently within.

04. It is not essential to understand the matter of Allaah's decree. [T / F]

FILL IN THE BLANK QUESTIONS

[Enter the correct individual word to complete the sentences from today's content.]

8 min

05. Allaah has given us _____ of will to chose what we say and do.

06. Allaah has given humans the _____ to choose how to behave in both our religious and worldly affairs.

07. People's work and efforts, their wealth, their life spans only occur _____ the will of Allaah.

08. Human beings' capacity to obey Allaah or commit sins is according to Allaah's _____.

COMPREHENSIVE UNDERSTANDING QUESTION

3-7min

[*]. Give a possible example of how the false understanding of someone believing that Allaah's decree compels them and removes their choices, can be an excuse for what they might do or not do in their life.

DAY - 06

TEACHER NOTES / CORRECTIONS

✳[/ *]

TEST YOUR UNDERSTANDING:

DAY - 07

4 min

TRUE & FALSE QUESTIONS

[Chose true or false for each individual sentence from today's content.]

01. Allaah tells us to seek intercession of the righteous in graves to bring our supplications closer to Him. [T / F]

02. There are holy objects that represent Allaah we can symbolically supplicate towards as Muslims. [T / F]

03. Allaah has taught us that we can get closer to Him through acts of obedience. [T / F]

04. The Prophet taught the Companions to seek the assistance of the righteous Muslims who had died, to come closer to Allaah. [T / F]

FILL IN THE BLANK QUESTIONS

[Enter the correct individual word to complete the sentences from today's content.]

8 min

05. The Arabic word _____ means that you direct to other than Allaah worship that should be for Him alone.

06. It is forbidden to direct any form of worship toward some part of Allaah's _____, including toward those who are dead in their graves.

07. All false means, such as asking the dead in graves, do not bring us closer to Allaah, but only _____ us from Him.

08. We should search for ways to gain closeness to Allaah through those acts of _____ He loves has legislated as permissible.

COMPREHENSIVE UNDERSTANDING QUESTION

3-7 min

[*]. Give a general example of the false practice of seeking closeness to Allaah through supplicating to things from His creation for intercession, which is found among other religions outside of Islaam.

TEACHER NOTES / CORRECTIONS

*[/ *]

TEST YOUR UNDERSTANDING:

4 min

TRUE & FALSE QUESTIONS

[Chose true or false for each individual sentence from today's content.]

01. The Companion 'Umar ibn al-Khattab approved of new [T / F] innovations in Islaam.

02. We can engage in spiritual activities at the graves of the [T / F] righteous, if a knowledgeable sheikh teaches us this.

03. The Prophet's statements indicate that all innovations are [T / F] blameworthy misguidance and harmful to us.

04. Beneficial acts such as printing the Qur'an in a single volume [T / F] are not considered religious innovations.

8 min

FILL IN THE BLANK QUESTIONS

[Enter the correct individual word to complete the sentences from today's content.]

05. The Prophet, may the praise and salutations of Allaah be upon him, said, *{... every innovation is a going _____.}*

06. The Prophet, may the praise and salutations of Allaah be upon him, said, *{... And _____ of newly invented matters}*

07. The Prophet, may the praise and salutations of Allaah be upon him, said, *{The one who invents something new in this religion of ours, that is not of it, that matter is _____.}*

08. The statement of 'Umar, about the nightly taraaweeh prayer in the month of Ramadhaan, is understood from the _____ standpoint only.

COMPREHENSIVE UNDERSTANDING QUESTION

3-7min

[*]. Discuss a general religious innovation, found among any other religion outside of Islaam, that the original teaching of that religion did not speak about, support, or call to.

DAY - 08

TEACHER NOTES / CORRECTIONS

*[/ *]

TEST YOUR UNDERSTANDING:

TRUE & FALSE QUESTIONS

[Chose true or false for each individual sentence from today's content.]

01. New ways of thinking from the "new age" movement should be [T / F] embraced by Muslims as part of their way of life.

02. The Messenger of Allaah never spoke about divisions among [T / F] Muslims.

03. Religious innovations all share some similar important [T / F] characteristics.

04. We can accept new principles or practices in Islaam if we all [T / F] agree upon them.

FILL IN THE BLANK QUESTIONS

[Enter the correct individual word to complete the sentences from today's content.]

05. Muslims must _____ and examine their statements, actions, and acts of ritual worship against the Qur'aan and Sunnah.

06. Muslims should beautify whatever they do and say by making sure it is _____ by what Allaah has said and what His Messenger has said.

07. Blameworthy innovation are often matters connected to ritual worship among the people, by which they intend _____ to their Lord.

08. Every agreement or covenant which opposes the guidance of revealed Sharee'ah is something that must be _____.

COMPREHENSIVE UNDERSTANDING QUESTION

3-7 min

[*]. Briefly describe any methodology or movement that has influence among Muslims in our century, which has something new within it lacking a clear basis in the way of the Prophet and his Companions.

DAY - 09

TEACHER NOTES / CORRECTIONS

✳[/ *]

TEST YOUR UNDERSTANDING:

4 min

TRUE & FALSE QUESTIONS

[Chose true or false for each individual sentence from today's content.]

01. There are historical followers of the original message of Prophet 'Isaa who will be in Paradise. [T / F]

02. There is a saved sect of Muslims always present in the world. [T / F]

03. There are many groups and sects that have developed new false forms of what they call Islaam. [T / F]

04. It is acceptable to Allaah that each sect cling to its own developed beliefs and practices. [T / F]

8 min

FILL IN THE BLANK QUESTIONS

[Enter the correct individual word to complete the sentences from today's content.]

05. The saved sect are those who _____ together and stand steadfastly upon that revealed truth which the Messenger of Allaah came with.

06. The saved sect are _____ by their connection to the noble hadeeth narrations.

07. It is important to look closely and examine critically every sect that puts forth a _____ that it is the saved sect.

08. The _____ and scale for judging and weighing is the tremendous Qur'aan and the pure Sunnah in relation to every single sect.

COMPREHENSIVE UNDERSTANDING QUESTION

3-7min

[*]. Briefly discuss any misguided sect and explain one religious matter they have strayed away from the guidance of the Prophet Muhammad regarding.

DAY - 10

TEACHER NOTES / CORRECTIONS

✱[/ *]

TEST YOUR UNDERSTANDING:

4 min

DAY - 11

TRUE & FALSE QUESTIONS

[Chose true or false for each individual sentence from today's content.]

01. Every human has been commanded to worship Allaah alone [T / F] with no associates.

02. Every Muslim should understand the importance of glorifying [T / F] and worshiping Allaah alone, separate from everything other than Him.

03. When Muslims differ with each other we should simply [T / F] cooperate on what we accept and excuse the differences.

04. There are some rulings or issues that the scholars make that [T / F] some of them are not correct in.

FILL IN THE BLANK QUESTIONS

[Enter the correct individual word to complete the sentences from today's content.]

8 min

05. Allaah created His creations to worship Him alone without _____ any others in that worship with Him.

06. Muslims must specifically direct toward Allaah their supplications, and the fear and hope in their _____.

07. The Qur'aan, the Book of Allaah contains _____ and light.

08. Muslims to give attention to the Book of Allaah, _____ it, and seeking to understand it.

COMPREHENSIVE UNDERSTANDING QUESTION

3-7min

[*]. Discuss one aspect of why Ibraheem is a model for us as Muslims, and give a possible example of the opposite of that reason.

DAY - 11

TEACHER NOTES / CORRECTIONS

TEST YOUR UNDERSTANDING:

TRUE & FALSE QUESTIONS

[Chose true or false for each individual sentence from today's content.]

01. A Muslim is required by the Sunnah to adopt a specific school [T / F] of thought.

02. When a Muslim is aware of the ruling for something in Islaam [T / F] he should search in the Qur'aan.

03. Every Muslim should gain authentic knowledge, to the degree [T / F] they are able, about matters in their practice.

04. A students of knowledge should review the statements of the [T / F] scholars.

FILL IN THE BLANK QUESTIONS

[Enter the correct individual word to complete the sentences from today's content.]

05. It is not something required upon a Muslim to _____ themselves to a specific historical school of jurisprudence.

06. It is something required upon every Muslim is that they _____ for the truth of matters and consider the evidences about them.

07. The person who is ignorant of some matter should _____ the people of knowledge.

08. A male student of knowledge or a female student knowledge should consider the Sharee'ah _____ as much as they are able.

COMPREHENSIVE UNDERSTANDING QUESTION

3-7min

[*].   Discuss a possible reason why knowing where a scholar takes his information or knowledge from is important is accepting the rulings and guidance that scholar offers you.

DAY - 12

TEACHER NOTES / CORRECTIONS

[/]

TEST YOUR UNDERSTANDING:

4min

TRUE & FALSE QUESTIONS

[Chose true or false for each individual sentence from today's content.]

01. The entire world and everything within it is completely cursed. [T / F]

02. The general believing men and the believing women are those [T / F] engaged in what Allaah is pleased with.

03. The leaving of some matters is something that can be pleasing [T / F] to Allaah.

04. The people involved with spreading authentic knowledge are [T / F] not included in what the world has of scorned matters.

8min

FILL IN THE BLANK QUESTIONS

[Enter the correct individual word to complete the sentences from today's content.]

05. The majority of what is in the world _____ people from concern for the Hereafter.

06. The general situation of the believing men and women and their righteousness are part of what results from the _____ of Allaah.

07. The teachers with a concern for the Sharee'ah guidance are _____ from this general description of scorned matters.

08. The establishment of the obligatory prayer and fasting and what is similar to it of beneficial actions is _____.

DAY - 13

COMPREHENSIVE UNDERSTANDING QUESTION

3-7 min

[*].   Give a brief specific example of how a Muslim can be from among the people whom Allaah is clearly pleased with through the activities they are occupied with in this world.

DAY - 13

TEACHER NOTES / CORRECTIONS

[/]

TEST YOUR UNDERSTANDING:

4 min

TRUE & FALSE QUESTIONS

[Chose true or false for each individual sentence from today's content.]

01. Sufism was not practiced by the Companions of the Prophet. [T / F]

02. Every matter of worship people consider good among the Sufee [T / F] groups is already found in the authentic Sunnah.

03. It is not necessary to take acts of worship only from revealed [T / F] guidance.

04. Allaah commanded us to follow whatever path we feel brings [T / F] us towards Him.

8 min

FILL IN THE BLANK QUESTIONS

[Enter the correct individual word to complete the sentences from today's content.]

05. The developed paths of the different Sufees groups or orders do not have an evidenced basis within the _____ Sharee'ah.

06. Whatever partially correct acts of remembrance the Sufees practice are _____ from the guidance of the Book of Allaah and the Sunnah.

07. It is obligatory upon the people who connect themselves to Islaam is that they generally take their _____ directly from the Book of Allaah and the Sunnah.

08. The Prophet made clear that sound acts of worship were his own actions and statements, then his _____ further explained them.

COMPREHENSIVE UNDERSTANDING QUESTION

3-7min

[*]. Discuss why those who adhere to the Sunnah believe that every form of worship, including dhikr or remembrance of Allaah, is already perfected in Islaam practiced of the first Muslims?

DAY - 14

TEACHER NOTES / CORRECTIONS

✳[/ *]

TEST YOUR UNDERSTANDING:

TRUE & FALSE QUESTIONS

[Chose true or false for each individual sentence from today's content.]

4 min

01. There are steps needed to generally benefit from the various [T / F] books of Sharee'ah knowledge.

02. The scholars we should study with have certain needed [T / F] characteristics.

03. The best way to study the Qur'aan is recitation, contemplation, [T / F] along with scholastic study.

04. We can simply rely on ourselves and ponder to figure out the [T / F] meaning of verses we do not fully understand.

DAY - 15

FILL IN THE BLANK QUESTIONS

[Enter the correct individual word to complete the sentences from today's content.]

8 min

05. If someone has not learned what would enable him to correctly read through books, he will not gain _____ from simply reading.

06. Studying alone will undoubtedly cause you to make many _____.

07. A Muslim will not benefit in a significant and _____ way except if he has studied with the people of knowledge.

08. If a Muslim has not studied general principles of Sharee'ah knowledge, he will often not _____ the source texts properly.

COMPREHENSIVE UNDERSTANDING QUESTION

3-7min

[*]. Discuss some possible ways a Muslim today can build a study program for themselves and their family in a beneficial way. What specific types of resources might they take from to learn and study?

DAY - 15

TEACHER NOTES / CORRECTIONS

*[/ *]

TEST YOUR UNDERSTANDING:

TRUE & FALSE QUESTIONS

[Chose true or false for each individual sentence from today's content.]

01. Praising the scholars in front of the people only contains good.   [T / F]

02. There is no danger in praising someone, if you are only truthful   [T / F]
and accurate.

03. The previous nations fell into the mistake of excessively praising   [T / F]
the righteous.

04. A scholar should inwardly and outwardly have a dislike of   [T / F]
being praised.

FILL IN THE BLANK QUESTIONS

[Enter the correct individual word to complete the sentences from today's content.]

05. The Prophet prohibited the Muslims from having _____ towards
him.

06. _____ the scholars can be a cause for extremism and bias towards
them.

07. Students praising their scholar can lead to the evil of him _____
having arrogance, and being prideful.

08. There is no harm in a small amount of praise which is intended to
_____ someone upon goodness.

COMPREHENSIVE UNDERSTANDING QUESTION

3-7 min

[*].   What are some of the possible benefits of properly using limited praise in a restricted way with those who are striving to learn Sharee'ah knowledge to benefit themselves and hopefully their communities?

DAY - 16

TEACHER NOTES / CORRECTIONS

✳[/ *]

TEST YOUR UNDERSTANDING:

TRUE & FALSE QUESTIONS

[Chose true or false for each individual sentence from today's content.]

4 min

01. Muslims are allowed to use things that cause us harm if we   [T / F]
     personally choose to.

02. Everything Allaah said is permissible is known to be good.   [T / F]

03. There is no proof that smoking is harmful to those who engage   [T / F]
     in it.

04. We cannot use tobacco for smoking ourselves but selling it to   [T / F]
     others to smoke is acceptable.

DAY - 17

FILL IN THE BLANK QUESTIONS

[Enter the correct individual word to complete the sentences from today's content.]

8 min

05. Allaah has ennobled mankind and commanded humanity with that
     which _____ him.

06. Allaah has _____ human beings from that which causes us harm.

07. A Muslim must distance himself from _____ consumed which
     causes him harm.

08. The practice of smoking is something both _____ and filthy.

COMPREHENSIVE UNDERSTANDING QUESTION

3-7min

[*]. Discuss one possible or common reason that people start smoking, and how that could be avoided.

DAY - 17

TEACHER NOTES / CORRECTIONS

[/]

TEST YOUR UNDERSTANDING:

TRUE & FALSE QUESTIONS

[Chose true or false for each individual sentence from today's content.]

4 min

01. We should only rely upon our own determination to stay away [T / F] from sins.

02. It is important to be someone who repents from mistakes [T / F] quickly.

03. Our friends and companions are truly important in terms of [T / F] struggling to avoid sins.

04. There is no real benefit on thinking about our sins and our [T / F] repentance from them when trying to be a good Muslim.

FILL IN THE BLANK QUESTIONS

[Enter the correct individual word to complete the sentences from today's content.]

8 min

05. True repentance _____ those transgressions that came before it.

06. Islaam removes those sins that occurred _____ someone becomes Muslim.

07. If a Muslim _____ repents to Allaah again, He will erase that sin from you again.

08. Every Muslim must struggle and work hard with themselves to _____ falling into sins.

COMPREHENSIVE UNDERSTANDING QUESTION

3-7min

[*]. Discuss some possible additional strategies that might be helpful in staying away from committing sins specific to modern technologies.

DAY - 18

TEACHER NOTES / CORRECTIONS

✱[/ *]

TEST YOUR UNDERSTANDING:

4 min

TRUE & FALSE QUESTIONS

[Chose true or false for each individual sentence from today's content.]

01. We can only repent at certain times when Allaah then accepts [T / F] it.

02. After fulfilling the conditions of repentance we should feel [T / F] confident that it was accepted.

03. We should hope for good from Allaah after choosing to repent [T / F] from transgressions.

04. When we embrace Islaam our past sins remain with us. [T / F]

DAY - 19

8 min

FILL IN THE BLANK QUESTIONS

[Enter the correct individual word to complete the sentences from today's content.]

05. The one who repents from a transgression is like someone who _____ engaged in it.

06. A Muslim should inwardly have a firm resolve to not _____ to those sins after repentance.

07. A Muslim should always have the _____ suspicion of their Lord who is the Most Perfect and the Most High, and turn towards repentance.

08. If you have done an injustice to someone then returning their _____ to them is part of correctly repenting.

COMPREHENSIVE UNDERSTANDING QUESTION

3-7 min

[*]. Why is it important to understand that repentance has conditions? Give a possible example of a repentance which is done incorrectly.

DAY - 19

TEACHER NOTES / CORRECTIONS

*[/ *]

TEST YOUR UNDERSTANDING:

TRUE & FALSE QUESTIONS

[Chose true or false for each individual sentence from today's content.]

4 min

01. It is not likely that Muslim might imitate others in a harmful   [T / F] way.

02. Muslim should benefit from advances in technology and similar   [T / F] developed systems.

03. There are neutral matters related to professional organization   [T / F] that are acceptable for Muslims.

04. The Muslims being equipped for self-defense of their lands and   [T / F] nations is something beneficial.

FILL IN THE BLANK QUESTIONS

[Enter the correct individual word to complete the sentences from today's content.]

8 min

DAY - 20

05. It is obligatory on a Muslim to be a _____ individual upon guidance.

06. The Messenger of Allaah warned the Muslim Ummah against following the patterns and ways of the _____ nations.

07. The Muslim should not imitate others whether this be in their character, their actions, their speech, or their _____.

08. There are mutual general matters through which everyone collectively benefits from, that are not considered _____ imitation.

COMPREHENSIVE UNDERSTANDING QUESTION

3-7 min

[*].   Discuss a possible benefit, in their interaction with those who are non-Muslims, of the Muslims being distinct in the various aspects of life and culture?

DAY - 20

TEACHER NOTES / CORRECTIONS

*[/ *]

TEST YOUR UNDERSTANDING:

4 min

TRUE & FALSE QUESTIONS

[Chose true or false for each individual sentence from today's content.]

01. We should not have any connection at all to the non-Muslims around us. [T / F]

02. It is allowed for a Muslim to offer general condolences to a non-Muslim on the death of a family member. [T / F]

03. The non-Muslim living next to you should not be treated well, as your neighbor. [T / F]

04. There is little benefit in trying to clarify misconceptions and call others to Islaam. [T / F]

FILL IN THE BLANK QUESTIONS

[Enter the correct individual word to complete the sentences from today's content.]

8 min

DAY - 21

05. A Muslim should, to the degree of his _____, explain to those non-Muslims around him the meaning of Islaam.

06. It is _____ to invite a non-Muslim to one's home for a gathering or meal there and explain aspects about Islaam.

07. A Muslim does not oppress or harm his non-Muslim _____, neither in his self, wealth, or honor.

08. It is impermissible for a Muslim to participate in the _____ of non-Muslim festivals.

COMPREHENSIVE UNDERSTANDING QUESTION

3-7 min

[*].   What is a possible example of ignoring or neglecting the guidance of Islaam in dealing with non-Muslims. Additionally, what is a possible example of extremism against the guidance of Islaam in dealing with them?

DAY - 21

TEACHER NOTES / CORRECTIONS

✳[/ *]

TEST YOUR UNDERSTANDING:

4 min

TRUE & FALSE QUESTIONS

[Chose true or false for each individual sentence from today's content.]

01. There are things we should consider when we take people as friends. [T / F]

02. People who engage in sins we should be neutral towards, not being close to nor far away from. [T / F]

03. There are general reasons for helping someone of the opposite gender that Islaam permits. [T / F]

04. We can help someone for religious reasons, no matter how that is done. [T / F]

8 min

DAY - 22

FILL IN THE BLANK QUESTIONS

[Enter the correct individual word to complete the sentences from today's content.]

05. We can take as friends people who _____ sin and transgress.

06. Companionship with someone of the opposite gender, and taking them as friend is a significant _____.

07. We should avoid all friendship with the opposite gender that are questionable or which involves _____ in some form with one of them, or some wrongdoing.

08. It is not permissible to engage in anything which will cause you to slip into immoral speech or behavior and lead you towards matters which _____

COMPREHENSIVE UNDERSTANDING QUESTION

3-7min

[*]. Discuss some of the reasons there might be acceptable cooperation of various people of opposite genders at a masjid or Islamic center. How should that be conducted according to the guidance of Islaam?

DAY - 22

TEACHER NOTES / CORRECTIONS

---

*[/ *]

TEST YOUR UNDERSTANDING:

4 min

TRUE & FALSE QUESTIONS

[Chose true or false for each individual sentence from today's content.]

01. It is acceptable to use a small amount of alcohol for flavoring [T / F] when cooking.
02. If an intoxicant is a natural component of food or a plant it is [T / F] acceptable.
03. Muslim are prohibited from intentionally harming themselves. [T / F]
04. Intoxicant generally cause more good than harm between [T / F] people.

8 min

FILL IN THE BLANK QUESTIONS

[Enter the correct individual word to complete the sentences from today's content.]

05. The Messenger of Allaah prohibited _____ found in any substance.
06. There are significant forms of _____ connected to the consumption of intoxicants.
07. Any substance which causes definitive harm through using it, it is _____ for Muslims.
08. Allaah has made prohibited for us whatever harms our _____ or physical bodies.

DAY - 23

COMPREHENSIVE UNDERSTANDING QUESTION

3-7min

[*].   Briefly discuss one social harm not mentioned from the use of intoxicants and drugs in society.

TEACHER NOTES / CORRECTIONS

DAY - 23

[/]

TEST YOUR UNDERSTANDING:

4 min

TRUE & FALSE QUESTIONS

[Chose true or false for each individual sentence from today's content.]

01. Because some people say there is a difference of opinion then music is permitted for Muslims. [T / F]

02. This is a description of blameworthy speech in the Qur'aan that some of the Companions and scholars held included music. [T / F]

03. There are forms of clothing once clearly prohibited in Islaam that some people wrongly consider now acceptable for Muslims. [T / F]

04. Regarding intoxicants, the Prophet considered the many different people involved with it as wrongdoers and sinful. [T / F]

8 min

FILL IN THE BLANK QUESTIONS

[Enter the correct individual word to complete the sentences from today's content.]

05. The general ruling about music and similar forms of musical entertainment, in all forms, is that it is _____.

06. The Prophet informed us that in the later times there would be people who drink wine and simply call it another _____.

07. The Muslims should not simply copy and _____ the disbelievers in these issues of entertainment.

08. Many people have made musical instruments _____ by calling it by other different names.

DAY - 24

COMPREHENSIVE UNDERSTANDING QUESTION

3-7min

[*]. Give an example of a common excuse that some people often give for engaging in something, which is actually clearly prohibited in Islaam.

DAY - 24

TEACHER NOTES / CORRECTIONS

*[/ *]

TEST YOUR UNDERSTANDING:

TRUE & FALSE QUESTIONS

[Chose true or false for each individual sentence from today's content.]

01. All television programs are allowed because it is just something from culture. [T / F]

02. Modern media can be used to properly teach aspects of the culture and history of Islaam. [T / F]

03. Whatever is watched as media shows must only be about to the Qur'aan and Sunnah. [T / F]

04. Muslims must consider the long term effects of the media they watch. [T / F]

FILL IN THE BLANK QUESTIONS

[Enter the correct individual word to complete the sentences from today's content.]

05. There is no harm if television series and other programs spread that which _____ the people in their religious or general affairs.

06. There is no harm if television series on modern subjects, or matters that are aspects of what is acknowledged to be something _____.

07. Television series and similar media which display indecent images or musical entertainment are not _____.

08. Media and television programs that corrupt the _____ of a Muslim, may even lead to the corruption of their essential beliefs.

COMPREHENSIVE UNDERSTANDING QUESTION

3-7min

[*]. Give three examples of modern types or titles of programs that might be permissible for a Muslim to watch through the internet channel.

TEACHER NOTES / CORRECTIONS

DAY - 25

TEST YOUR UNDERSTANDING:

4 min

TRUE & FALSE QUESTIONS

[Chose true or false for each individual sentence from today's content.]

01. Muslims who do not speak Arabic should focus on reading the   [T / F]
    Qur'aan to gain the reward of reciting each letter.

02. There are works of the scholars that will help the seeker of   [T / F]
    knowledge better understand the Qur'aan.

03. If we cannot understand it fully there is little reason to both   [T / F]
    recite and read the meanings of the Qur'aan.

04. There are several excellent Arabic sources of transmitted   [T / F]
    commentary that explain the Qur'aan properly.

8 min

FILL IN THE BLANK QUESTIONS

[Enter the correct individual word to complete the sentences from today's content.]

05. It is permissible for a believing man or a believing woman to recite the
    Qur'aan even if they do not speak _____.

06. The books of the Arabic language are a valid resource in helping to
    _____ the meaning of the Qur'aan.

07. The believing woman should understand what is meant by the verses of
    the Qur'aan so that she can _____ upon them.

08. Allaah encourages us and inspires us to _____ and contemplate
    His words.

DAY - 26

COMPREHENSIVE UNDERSTANDING QUESTION

3-7min

[*]. Discuss one possible significant effect of listening or reading the authentic translated meanings of the Qur'aan can have in strengthening the Islaam of a new Muslim.

TEACHER NOTES / CORRECTIONS

DAY - 26

*[/ *]

TEST YOUR UNDERSTANDING:

4 min

TRUE & FALSE QUESTIONS

[Chose true or false for each individual sentence from today's content.]

01. There are different statements or remembrances for different   [T / F]
    times of the day.

02. A Muslim should not engage in remembrance when doing   [T / F]
    general non-religious work.

03. It is better the say those remembrances affirmed in the Sunnah   [T / F]
    for after salaat, right after its performance.

04. The authentic supplications and dhikr of the Prophet help   [T / F]
    cultivate our hearts in a way pleasing to Allaah.

8 min

FILL IN THE BLANK QUESTIONS

[Enter the correct individual word to complete the sentences from today's content.]

05. Every statement of remembrance should have a _____ in the
    Sharee'ah.

06. Some statements of remembrance are to be said in the early part of the
    _____.

07. It is _____ to say general remembrance in that place and work
    endeavor someone is engaged in.

08. The remembrances found in the Sunnah fostering _____ within
    the heart.

DAY - 27

COMPREHENSIVE UNDERSTANDING QUESTION

3-7 min

[*]. Discuss a possible way the use of affirmed supplications and authentic remembrances from the Sunnah, throughout the day, can strengthen us as Muslims seeking Allaah's pleasure.

TEACHER NOTES / CORRECTIONS

DAY - 27

∗[/ ∗]

TEST YOUR UNDERSTANDING:

4 min

TRUE & FALSE QUESTIONS

[Chose true or false for each individual sentence from today's content.]

01. A Muslim husband can ask his wife to do permissible customary things in the home. [T / F]

02. A Muslim wife should obey her husband in everything he tells her to do. [T / F]

03. The rights of the Muslim wife are whatever customs says they should be. [T / F]

04. Both the husband and the wife should strive to give each other their rights as defined in Islaam and work to strengthen their marriage together. [T / F]

FILL IN THE BLANK QUESTIONS

[Enter the correct individual word to complete the sentences from today's content.]

8 min

05. It is _____ upon a Muslim wife to obey her Muslim husband in matters that are acceptable in Islaam.

06. If a Muslim husband tells his wife to do something which is _____ then she should neither listen nor obey to that.

07. The Prophet, said, *{Fear Allaah with regard to women, for you have taken them as a _____ from Allaah...}*

08. A Muslim husband being _____ without the proper causes only ends up being a cause for eventual separation.

COMPREHENSIVE UNDERSTANDING QUESTION

3-7 min

[*]. Discuss one possible challenge Muslims, striving to practice Islaam today, often face related to marriage.

TEACHER NOTES / CORRECTIONS

TEST YOUR UNDERSTANDING:

4 min

TRUE & FALSE QUESTIONS

[Chose true or false for each individual sentence from today's content.]

01. We must know that Allaah has an important role in the success [T / F]
of every effort we undertake.

02. It is acceptable to wait for good to reach us without working [T / F]
for it in any way.

03. It is not permissible to not work for your livelihood when this [T / F]
is needed and possible.

04. Maryam, the mother of the Prophet 'Isaa, received blessing [T / F]
from Allah without any efforts on her part.

8 min

FILL IN THE BLANK QUESTIONS

[Enter the correct individual word to complete the sentences from today's content.]

05. Trusting in Allaah includes _____ specific matters.

06. One aspect of trusting in Allaah is to put into effect _____
towards the causes to accomplish matters.

07. It is not permissible for a believer to ignore the need to engage in the
_____ for bringing about desired matters.

08. Allaah can direct clear miracles towards some of his close associates and
devoted _____.

COMPREHENSIVE UNDERSTANDING QUESTION

3-7 min

[*].   Give an specific example of a permissible goal a Muslim might have, and briefly discuss how they would fulfill both of the matters of trusting in Allaah for success in achieving that.

_____

_____

_____

_____

_____

_____

_____

_____

_____

_____

_____

_____

_____

_____

_____

_____

_____

_____

TEACHER NOTES / CORRECTIONS

_____

_____

_____

_____

DAY - 29

❋[/*]

TEST YOUR UNDERSTANDING:

4 min

TRUE & FALSE QUESTIONS

[Chose true or false for each individual sentence from today's content.]

01. There are conditions for circumcision to be performed on a   [T / F]
    male after they enter Islaam.

02. A person changing his name helps other people recognize that   [T / F]
    he is now a Muslim.

03. A revert or convert to Islaam should always be informed about   [T / F]
    all of the obligations within Islaam right away.

04. If a qualified doctor stated that there is a danger in circumcision   [T / F]
    for an older man, then the obligation is removed.

8 min

FILL IN THE BLANK QUESTIONS

[Enter the correct individual word to complete the sentences from today's content.]

05. If that person embracing Islaam has a name which is not considered
    appropriate then he should _____ his name after embracing
    Islaam.

06. Names that indicate the worship of other than Allaah, such as what
    means worshiper of the Messiah, and worshiper of something in nature
    are not _____ for a Muslim to keep.

07. If there is nothing to prevent that, then when an older man embraces
    Islaam what is _____ is that he gets circumcised, if that was not
    previously done.

08. We should not mention the matter of performing circumcision if that
    will cause someone to turn _____ from Islaam.

COMPREHENSIVE UNDERSTANDING QUESTION

3-7min

[*]. Discuss any essential matter from the most important beliefs that a new Muslim should learn when they first enter into Islaam.

TEACHER NOTES / CORRECTIONS

THE NAKHLAH
EDUCATIONAL SERIES:

MISSION

The Purpose of the 'Nakhlah Educational Series' is to contribute to the present knowledge based efforts which enable Muslim individuals, families, and communities to understand and learn Islaam and then to develop withi,n and truly live, Islaam. Our commitment and goal is to contribute beneficial publications and works that:

Firstly, reflect the priority, message and methodology of all the prophets and messengers sent to humanity, meaning that single revealed message which embodies the very purpose of life, and of human creation. As Allaah the Most High has said,

We sent a Messenger to every nation ordering them that they should worship Allaah alone, obey Him and make their worship purely for Him, and that they should avoid everything worshipped besides Allaah. So from them there were those whom Allaah guided to His religion, and there were those who were unbelievers for whom misguidance was ordained. So travel through the land and see the destruction that befell those who denied the Messengers and disbelieved.—(Surah an-Nahl: 36)

Sheikh Rabee'a ibn Haadee al-Madkhalee in his work entitled, 'The Methodology of the Prophets in Calling to Allaah, That is the Way of Wisdom and Intelligence.' explains the essential, enduring message of all the prophets:

"So what was the message which these noble, chosen men, may Allaah's praises and salutations of peace be upon them all, brought to their people? Indeed their mission encompassed every matter of good and distanced and restrained every matter of evil. They brought forth to mankind everything needed for their well-being and happiness in this world and the Hereafter. There is nothing good except that they guided the people towards it, and nothing evil except that they warned the people against it. ...

This was the message found with all of the Messengers; that they should guide to every good and warn against every evil. However where did they start, what did they begin with, and what did they concentrate upon? There are a number of essentials, basic principles, and fundamentals which all their calls were founded upon, and which were the starting point for calling the people to Allaah. These fundamental points and principles are: 1. The worship of Allaah alone without any associates 2. The sending of prophets to guide creation 3. The belief in the resurrection and the life of the Hereafter

These three principles are the area of commonality and unity within their calls, and stand as the fundamental principles which they were established upon. These principles are given the greatest importance in the Qur'aan and are fully explained in it. They are also its most important purpose upon which it centers and which it continually mentions. It further quotes intellectual and observable *proofs for them in all its chapters as well as within most of its accounts of previous nations and given examples.*

This is known to those who have full understanding, and are able to consider carefully and comprehend well. All the Books revealed by Allaah have given great importance to these points and all of the various revealed laws of guidance are agreed upon them. And the most important and sublime of these three principles, and the most fundamental of them all, is directing one's worship only towards Allaah alone, the Blessed and the Most High."

Today one finds that there are indeed many paths, groups, and organizations apparently presenting themselves as representing Islaam, which struggle to put forth an outwardly pleasing appearance to the general Muslims; but when their methods are placed upon the precise scale of conforming to priorities and methodology of the message of the prophets sent by Allaah, they can only be recognized as deficient paths- not simply in practice but in principle- leading not to success, but rather only to inevitable failure.

As Sheikh Saaleh al-Fauzaan, may Allaah preserve him, states in his introduction to the same above-mentioned work on the methodology of all the prophets,

"So whichever call is not built upon these foundations, and whatever methodology is not from the methodology of the Messengers - then it will be frustrated and fail, and it will be effort and toil without any benefit. The clearest proofs of this are those present-day groups and organizations which set out a methodology and program for themselves and their efforts of calling the people to Islaam which is different from the methodology of the Messengers. These groups have neglected the importance of the people having the correct belief and creed - except for a very few of them - and instead call for the correction of side-issues."

There can be no true success in any form for us as individuals, families, or larger communities without making the encompassing worship of Allaah alone, with no partners or associates, the very and only foundation of our lives. It is necessary that each individual knowingly choose to base his life upon that same foundation taught by all the prophets and messengers sent by the Lord of all the worlds, rather than simply delving into the assorted secondary concerns and issues invited to by the various numerous parties, innovated movements, and groups. Indeed Sheikh al-Albaanee, may Allaah have mercy upon him, stated:[1]

"...We unreservedly combat against this way of having various different parties and groups. As this false way- of group or organizational allegiances - conforms to the statement of Allaah the Most High, ◈ **But they have broken their religion among them into sects, each group rejoicing in what is with it as its beliefs. And every party is pleased with whatever they stand with.** ◈—*(Surah al-Mu'minoon: 53) And in truth they are no separate groups and parties in Islaam itself. There is only one true party, as is stated in a verse in the Qur'an,* ◈ **Verily, it is the party of Allaah that will be the successful.** ◈—*(Surah al-Mujadilaah: 58). The party of Allaah are those people who stand with the Messenger of Allaah, may Allaah's praise and salutations be upon him, meaning that an individual proceeds upon the methodology of the Companions of the Messenger. Due to this we call for having sound knowledge of the Book and the Sunnah."*

---

[1]   Knowledge Based Issues & Sharee'ah Rulings: The Rulings of The Guiding Scholar Sheikh Muhammad Naasiruddeen al-Albaanee Made in the City of Medina & In the Emirates – [Emiratee Fatwa no 114. P.30]

TWO ESSENTIAL FOUNDATIONS

Secondly, building upon the above foundation, our commitment is to contributing publications and works which reflect the inherited message and methodology of the acknowledged scholars of the many various branches of Sharee'ah knowledge, who stood upon the straight path of preserved guidance in every century and time since the time of our Messenger, may Allaah's praise and salutations be upon him. These people of knowledge, who are the inheritors of the Final Messenger, have always adhered closely to the two revealed sources of guidance: the Book of Allaah and the Sunnah of the Messenger of Allaah- may Allaah's praise and salutations be upon him, upon the united consensus, standing with the body of guided Muslims in every century - preserving and transmitting the true religion generation after generation. Indeed the Messenger of Allaah, may Allaah's praise and salutations be upon him, informed us that, *{ A group of people amongst my Ummah will remain obedient to Allaah's orders. They will not be harmed by those who leave them nor by those who oppose them, until Allaah's command for the Last Day comes upon them while they remain on the right path. }*[2]

We live in an age in which the question frequently asked is, "*How do we make Islaam a reality?*" and perhaps the related and more fundamental question is, "*What is Islaam?*", such that innumerable different voices quickly stand to offer countless different conflicting answers through books, lectures, and every available form of modern media. Yet the only true course of properly understanding this question and its answer- for ourselves and our families -is to return to the criterion given to us by our beloved Messenger, may Allaah's praise and salutations be upon him. Indeed the Messenger of Allaah, may Allaah's praise and salutations be upon him, indicated in an authentic narration, clarifying the matter beyond doubt, that the only "Islaam" which enables one to be truly successful and saved in this world and the next is as he said, *{... that which I am upon and my Companions are upon today.}*[3] referring to that Islaam which stands upon unchanging revealed knowledge. While every other changed and altered form of Islaam, whether through some form of extremism or negligence, or through the addition or removal of something, regardless of whether that came from a good intention or an evil one- is not the religion that Allaah informed us about when He revealed, ❴ *This day, those who disbelieved have given up all hope of your religion; so fear them not, but fear Me. This day, I have perfected your religion for you, completed My Favor upon you, and have chosen for you Islaam as your religion.*❵ –(Surah al-Maa'idah: 3)

[2]   Authentically narrated in Saheeh al-Bukhaaree
[3]   Authentically narrated in Jaam'ea at-Tirmidhee

The guiding scholar Sheikh al-Albaanee, may have mercy upon him, said,

"...And specifically mentioning those among the callers who have taken upon themselves the guiding of the young Muslim generation upon Islaam, working to educate them with its education, and to socialize them with its culture. Yet they themselves have generally not attempted to unify their understanding of those matters about Islaam regarding which the people of Islaam today differ about so severely.

And the situation is certainly not as is falsely supposed by some individuals from among them who are heedless or negligent - that the differences that exist among them are only in secondary matters without entering into or affecting the fundamental issues or principles of the religion; and the examples to prove that this is not true are numerous and recognized by those who have studied the books of the many differing groups and sects, or by the one who has knowledge of the various differing concepts and beliefs held by the Muslims today." [4]

Similarly he, may Allaah have mercy upon him, explained:[5]

"Indeed, Islaam is the only solution, and this statement is something which the various different Islamic groups, organizations, and movements could never disagree about. And this is something which is from the blessings of Allaah upon the Muslims. However there are significant differences between the different Islamic groups, organizations, and movements that are present today regarding that domain which working within will bring about our rectification. What is that area of work to endeavor within, striving to restore a way of life truly reflecting Islaam, renewing that system of living which comes from Islaam, and in order to establish the Islamic government? The groups and movements significantly differ upon this issue or point. Yet we hold that it is required to begin with the matters of tasfeeyah —clarification, and tarbeeyah -education and cultivation, with both of them being undertaken together.

As if we were to start with the issue of governing and politics, then it has been seen that those who occupy themselves with this focus firstly possess beliefs which are clearly corrupted and ruined, and secondly that their personal behavior, from the aspect of conforming to Islaam, is very far from conforming to the actual guidance of the Sharee'ah. While those who first concern themselves with working just to unite the people and gather the masses together under a broad banner of the general term "Islaam," then it is seen that within the minds of those speakers who raise such calls -in reality there is in fact no actual clear understanding of what Islaam is. Moreover, the understanding they have of Islaam has no significant impact in starting to change and reform their own lives. Due to this reason, you find that many such individuals from here and there, who hold this perspective, are unable to truly realize or reflect Islaam, even in areas of their own personal lives in matters which it is in fact easily possible for them to implement. Such an individual holds that no one - regardless of whether it is because of his arrogance or pridefulness - can enter into directing him in an area of his personal life!

---

[4]   Mukhtasir al-'Uloo Lil'Alee al-Ghafaar, page 55

[5]   Quoted from the work, 'The Life of Sheikh al-Albaanee, His Influence in Present Day Fields of Sharee'ah Knowledge, & the Praise of the Scholars for Him.' volume 1 page 380-385

Yet at the same time these same individuals are raising their voices saying, "Judgment is only for Allaah!" and "It is required that judgment of affairs be according to what Allaah revealed." And this is indeed a true statement, but the one who does not possess something certainly cannot give or offer it to others. The majority of Muslims today have not established the judgment of Allaah fully upon themselves, yet they still seek from others to establish the judgment of Allaah within their governments...

...And I understand that this issue or subject is not immune from there being those who oppose our methodology of tasfeeyah and tarbeeyah. As there is the one who would say, "But establishing this tasfeeyah and tarbeeyah is a matter which requires many long years!" So, I respond by saying, this is not an important consideration in this matter, what is important is that we carry out what we have been commanded to do within our religion and by our Mighty Lord. What is important is that we begin by properly understanding our religion first and foremost. After this is accomplished then it will not be important whether the road itself is long or short.

And indeed, I direct this statement of mine towards those men who are callers to the religion among the Muslims, and towards the scholars and those who direct our affairs. I call for them to stand upon complete knowledge of true Islaam, and to fight against every form of negligence and heedlessness regarding the religion, and against differing and disputes, as Allaah has said, ❧***...and do not dispute with one another for fear that you lose courage and your strength departs*** ❧*—(Surah al-Anfaal: 46).*

The guiding scholar Sheikh Zayd al-Madkhalee, may Allaah protect him, stated in his writing, 'The Well Established Principles of the Way of the First Generations of Muslims: It's Enduring & Excellent Distinct Characteristics' that,

"From among these principles and characteristics is that the methodology of tasfeeyah -or clarification, and tarbeeyah -or education and cultivation- is clearly affirmed and established as a true way coming from the first three generations of Islaam, and is something well known to the people of true merit from among them, as is concluded by considering all the related evidence. What is intended by tasfeeyah, when referring to it generally, is clarifying that which is the truth from that which is falsehood, what is goodness from that which is harmful and corrupt, and when referring to its specific meanings, it is distinguishing the noble Sunnah of the Prophet and the people of the Sunnah from those innovated matters brought into the religion and the people who are supporters of such innovations.

As for what is intended by tarbeeyah, it is calling all of the creation to take on the manners and embrace the excellent character invited to by that guidance revealed to them by their Lord through His worshiper and Messenger Muhammad, may Allaah's praise and salutations be upon him; so that they might have good character, manners, and behavior. As without this they cannot have a good life, nor can they put right their present condition or their final destination. And we seek refuge in Allaah from the evil of not being able to achieve that rectification."

Thus the methodology of the people of standing upon the Prophet's Sunnah, and proceeding upon the 'way of the believers' in every century is reflected in a focus and concern with these two essential matters: tasfeeyah- or clarification of what is original, revealed message

from the Lord of all the worlds, and tarbeeyah- or education and raising of ourselves, our families, and our communities, and our lands upon what has been distinguished to be that true message and path.

METHODOLOGY:

The Roles of the Scholars & General Muslims In Raising the New Generation

The priority and focus of the 'Nakhlah Educational Series' is reflected within in the following statements of Sheikh al-Albaanee, may Allaah have mercy upon him:

"As for the other obligation, then I intend by this the education of the young generation upon Islaam purified from all of those impurities we have mentioned, giving them a correct Islamic education from their very earliest years, without any influence of a foreign, disbelieving education."[6]

"...And since the Messenger of Allaah, may Allaah's praise and salutations be upon him, has indicated that the only cure to remove this state of humiliation that we find ourselves entrenched within, is truly returning back to the religion, then it is clearly obligatory upon us - through the people of knowledge- to correctly and properly understand the religion in a way that conforms to the sources of the Book of Allaah and the Sunnah, and that we educate and raise a new virtuous, righteous generation upon this." [7]

It is essential, in discussing our perspective upon this obligation of raising the new generation of Muslims, that we highlight and bring attention to a required pillar of these efforts as indicated by Sheikh al-Albaanee, may Allaah have mercy upon him, and others- in the golden words, *"through the people of knowledge."* Something we commonly experience today is that many people have various incorrect understandings of the role that the scholars should have in the life of a Muslim, failing to understand the way in which they fulfill their position as the inheritors of the Messenger of Allaah, may Allaah's praise and salutations be upon him, and stand as those who preserve and enable us to practice the guidance of Islaam. Indeed, the noble Imaam Sheikh as-Sa'dee, may Allaah have mercy upon him, in his work, *"A Definitive and Clear Explanation of the Work 'A Triumph for the Saved Sect'"* [8], has explained this crucial issue with an extraordinary explanation full of remarkable benefits:

---

[6]   Silsilaat al-Hadeeth ad-Da'eefah, Introduction pg. 2
[7]   Clarification and Cultivation and the Need of the Muslims for Them
[8]   A Definitive and Clear Explanation of the Work 'A Triumph for the Saved Sect'" pages 237-240

"Section: Explaining the Conditions for These Two Source Texts to Suffice You -or the Finding of Sufficiency in these Two Sources of Revelation.

Overall the conditions needed to achieve this and bring it about return to two matters:

Firstly, the presence of the requirements necessary for achieving this; meaning a complete devotion to the Book and the Sunnah, and the putting forth of efforts both in seeking to understand their intended meanings, as well as in striving to be guided by them. What is required secondly is the pushing away of everything which prevents achieving this finding of sufficiency in them.

This is through having a firm determination to distance yourself from everything which contradicts these two source texts in what comes from the historical schools of jurisprudence, assorted various statements, differing principles and their resulting conclusions which the majority of people proceed upon. These matters which contradict the two sources of revelation include many affairs which, when the worshiper of Allaah repels them from himself and stands against them, the realm of his knowledge, understanding, and deeds then expands greatly. Through a devotion to them and a complete dedication towards these two sources of revelation, proceeding upon every path which assists one's understanding them, and receiving enlightenment from the light of the scholars and being guided by the guidance that they possess- you will achieve that complete sufficiency in them. And surely, in the positions they take towards the leading people of knowledge and the scholars, the people are three types of individuals:

The first of them is the one who goes to extremes in his attachment to the scholars. He makes their statements something which are infallible as if their words held the same position as those of the statements of the Messenger of Allaah, may Allaah's praise and salutations be upon him, as well as giving those scholars' statements precedence and predominance over the Book of Allaah and the Sunnah. This is despite the fact that every leading scholar who has been accepted by this Ummah was one who promoted and encouraged the following of the Book and the Sunnah, commanding the people not to follow their own statements nor their school of thought in anything which stood in opposition to the Book of Allaah and the Sunnah.

The second type is the one who generally rejects and invalidates the statements of the scholars and forbids the referring to the statements of the leading scholars of guidance and those people of knowledge who stand as brilliant lamps in the darkness. This type of person neither relies upon the light of discernment with the scholars, nor utilizes their stores of knowledge. Or even if perhaps they do so, they do not direct thanks towards them for this. And this manner and way prohibits them from tremendous good. Furthermore, that which motivates such individuals to proceed in this way is their falsely supposing that the obligation to follow the Messenger of Allaah, may Allaah's praise and salutations be upon him, and the giving of precedence to his statements over the statements of anyone else, requires that they do so without any reliance upon the statements of the Companions, or those who followed them in goodness, or those leading scholars of guidance within the Ummah. This is a glaring and extraordinary mistake.

Indeed the Companions and the people of knowledge are the means and the agency between the Messenger of Allaah, may Allaah's praise and salutations be upon him, and his Ummah- in the transmission and spreading of his Sunnah in regard to both its wording and texts, as well as its

meanings and understanding. Therefore the one who follows them in what they convey in this is guided through their understandings, receives knowledge from the light they possess, benefits from the conclusions they have derived from these sources -of beneficial meanings and explanations, as well as in relation to subtle

matters which scarcely occur to the minds of some of the other people of knowledge, or barely comes to be discerned by their minds. Consequently, from the blessing of Allaah upon this Ummah is that He has given them these guiding scholars who cultivate and educate them upon two clear types of excellent cultivation.

The first category is education from the direction of one's knowledge and understanding. They educate the Ummah upon the more essential and fundamental matters before the more complex affairs. They convey the meanings of the Book and the Sunnah to the minds and intellects of the people through efforts of teaching which rectifies, and through composing various beneficial books of knowledge which a worshiper doesn't even have the ability to adequately describe what is encompassed within them of aspects of knowledge and benefits. These works reflect the presence of a clear white hand in deriving guidance from the Book of Allaah and the Sunnah, and through the arrangement, detailed clarification, division and explanation, through the gathering together of explanations, comparisons, conditions, pillars, and explanations about that which prevents the fulfillment of matters, as well as distinguishing between differing meanings and categorizing various knowledge based benefits.

The second category is education from the direction of one's conduct and actions. They cultivate the peoples characters encouraging them towards every praiseworthy aspect of good character, through explaining its ruling and high status, and what benefits comes to be realized from it, clarifying the reasons and paths which enable one to attain it, as well as those affairs which prevent, delay, or hinder someone becoming one distinguished and characterized by it. Because they, in reality, are those who bring nourishment to the hearts and the souls; they are the doctors who treat the diseases of the heart and its defects. As such, they educate the people through their statements, and actions, as well as their general guided way. Therefore the scholars have a tremendous right over this Ummah. A portion of love and esteem, respect and honor, and thanks, are due to them because their merits and their various good efforts stand above every other right after establishing the right of Allaah, and the right of His Messenger, may Allaah's praise and salutations be upon him.

Because of this, the third group of individuals in respect to the scholars are those who have been guided to understand their true role and position, and establish their rights, thanking them for their virtues and merits, benefiting by taking from the knowledge they have, while acknowledging their rank and status. They understand that the scholars are not infallible and that their statements must stand in conformance to the statements of the Messenger of Allaah, may Allaah's praise and salutations be upon him, and that each one from among them has that which is from guidance, knowledge, and correctness in his statements taken and benefited from, while turning away from whatever in mistaken within it.

Yet such a scholar is not to be belittled for his mistake, as he stands as one who strove to reach the truth; therefore his mistake will be forgiven, and he should be thanked for his efforts. One clarifies what was stated by of any one of these leaders from among men, when it is recognized that

OUR MISSION & METHODOLOGY

it has some weakness or conflict to an evidence of the Sharee'ah, by explaining its weakness and the level of that weakness, without speaking evilly of the intention of those people of knowledge and religion, nor defaming them due to that error. Rather we say, as it is obligatory to say, "And those who came after them say: ❨

Our Lord! forgive us and our brethren who have preceded us in faith, and put not in our hearts any hatred against those who have believed. Our Lord! You are indeed full of kindness, Most Merciful. ❩ *-(Surah al-Hashr: 10).*

Accordingly, individuals of this third type are those who fulfill two different matters. They join together on one hand between giving precedence to the Book and the Sunnah over everything else, and, on the other hand, between comprehending the level and position of the scholars and the leading people of knowledge and guidance, and establishing this even if it is only done in regard to some of their rights upon us. So we ask Allaah to bless us to be from this type, and to make us from among the people of this third type, and to make us from those who love Him and love those who love Him, and those who love every action which brings us closer to everything He loves."

Upon this clarity regarding the proper understanding of our balanced position towards our guided Muslim scholars, consider the following words about the realm of work of the general people of faith, which explains our area of efforts and struggle as Muslim parents, found in the following statement by Sheikh Saaleh Fauzaan al-Fauzaan, may Allaah preserve him.

*"**Question: Some people mistakenly believe that calling to Allaah is a matter not to be undertaken by anyone else other than the scholars without exception, and that it is not something required for other than the scholars, according to that which they have knowledge of, to undertake any efforts of calling the people to Allaah. So what is your esteemed guidance regarding this?"***

The Sheikh responded by saying:[9]

"This is not a misconception, but is in fact a reality. The call to Allaah cannot be established except through those who are scholars, and I state this. Yet, certainly there are clear issues which every person understands. As such, every individual should enjoin the good and forbid wrongdoing according to the level of his understanding, such that he instructs and orders the members of his household to perform the ritual daily prayers and other matters that are clear and well known.

*Undertaking this is something mandatory and required even upon the common people, such that they must command their children to perform their prayers in the masjid. The Messenger of Allaah, may Allaah praise and salutations be upon him, said, { **Command you children to pray at seven, and beat them due to its negligence at ten.**} (Authentic narration found in Sunan Abu Dawood). And the Messenger of Allaah, may Allaah praise and salutations be upon him, said, { **Each one of you is a guardian or a shepherd, and each of you is responsible for those under his guardianship....**} (Authentic narration found in Saheeh al-Bukhaaree). So this is called guardianship, and this is also called enjoining the good and forbidding wrongdoing. The Messenger of Allaah, may Allaah praise and salutations be upon him, said, { **The one from among you who sees a wrong should change it with his hand, and if he is unable to do so, then with his tongue, and**}*

---

[9] Beneficial Responses to Questions About Modern Methodologies, Question 15, page 22

if he is not able to do this, then with his heart. } (Authentic narration found in Saheeh Muslim).

So in relation to the common person, that which it is required from him to endeavor upon is that he commands the members of his household-as well as others -with the proper performance of the ritual prayers, the obligatory charity, with generally striving to obey Allaah, to stay away from sins and transgressions, that he purify and cleanse his home from disobedience, and that he educate and cultivate his children upon the obedience of Allaah's commands. This is what is required from him, even if he is a general person, as these types of matters are from that which is understood by every single person. This is something which is clear and apparent.

But as for the matters of putting forth rulings and judgments regarding matters in the religion, or entering into clarifying issues of what is permissible and what is forbidden, or explaining what is considered associating others in the worship due to Allaah and what is properly worshiping Him alone without any partner- then indeed these are matters which cannot be established except by the scholars"

Similarly the guiding scholar Sheikh 'Abdul-'Azeez Ibn Baaz, may Allaah have mercy upon him, also emphasized this same overall responsibility:

"...It is also upon a Muslim that he struggles diligently in that which will place his worldly affairs in a good state, just as he must also strive in the correcting of his religious affairs and the affairs of his own family. The people of his household have a significant right over him that he strive diligently in rectifying their affair and guiding them towards goodness, due to the statement of Allaah, the Most Exalted, ❴ **Oh you who believe! Save yourselves and your families Hellfire whose fuel is men and stones** ❵ -(Surah at-Tahreem: 6)

So it is upon you to strive to correct the affairs of the members of your family. This includes your wife, your children- both male and female- and such as your own brothers. This concerns all of the people in your family, meaning you should strive to teach them the religion, guiding and directing them, and warning them from those matters Allaah has prohibited for us. Because you are the one who is responsible for them as shown in the statement of the Prophet, may Allaah's praise and salutations be upon him, { **Every one of you is a guardian, and responsible for what is in his custody. The ruler is a guardian of his subjects and responsible for them; a husband is a guardian of his family and is responsible for it; a lady is a guardian of her husband's house and is responsible for it, and a servant is a guardian of his master's property and is responsible for it....**} Then the Messenger of Allaah, may Allaah's praise and salutations be upon him, continued to say, {**...so all of you are guardians and are responsible for those under your authority.**} (Authentically narrated in Saheeh al-Bukhaaree & Muslim)

It is upon us to strive diligently in correcting the affairs of the members of our families, from the aspect of purifying their sincerity of intention for Allaah's sake alone in all of their deeds, and ensuring that they truthfully believe in and follow the Messenger of Allaah, may Allaah's praise and salutations be upon him, their fulfilling the prayer and the other obligations which Allaah the Most Exalted has commanded for us, as well as from the direction of distancing them from everything which Allaah has prohibited.

It is upon every single man and woman to give advice to their families about the fulfillment of what is obligatory upon them. Certainly, it is upon the woman as well as upon the man to perform this. In this way our homes become corrected and rectified in regard to the most important and essential matters. Allaah said to His Prophet, may Allaah's praise and salutations be upon him, ❧ **And enjoin the ritual prayers on your family...** ❧ (Surah Taha: 132) Similarly, Allaah the Most Exalted said to His prophet Ismaa'aeel, ❧ **And mention in the Book, Ismaa'aeel. Verily, he was true to what he promised, and he was a Messenger, and a Prophet. And he used to enjoin on his family and his people the ritual prayers and the obligatory charity, and his Lord was pleased with him.** ❧ -(Surah Maryam: 54-55)

As such, it is only proper that we model ourselves after the prophets and the best of people, and be concerned with the state of the members of our households. Do not be neglectful of them, oh worshipper of Allaah! Regardless of whether it is concerning your wife, your mother, father, grandfather, grandmother, your brothers, or your children; it is upon you to strive diligently in correcting their state and condition..." [10]

---

[10] Collection of Various Rulings and Statements- Sheikh 'Abdul-'Azeez Ibn 'Abdullah Ibn Baaz, Vol. 6, page 47

CONTENT & STRUCTURE:

We hope to contribute works which enable every striving Muslim who acknowledges the proper position of the scholars, to fulfill the recognized duty and obligation which lays upon each one of us to bring the light of Islaam into our own lives as individuals, as well as into our homes and among our families. Towards this goal we are committed to developing educational publications and comprehensive educational curricula -through cooperation with and based upon the works of the scholars of Islaam and the students of knowledge. Works which, with the assistance of Allaah, the Most High, we can utilize to educate and instruct ourselves, our families and our communities upon Islaam in both principle and practice. The publications and works of the Nakhlah Educational Series are divided into the following categories:

Basic / Elementary: Ages 4-11   *Secondary: Ages 11-14*

High School: Ages 14- Young Adult   *General: Young Adult –Adult*

Supplementary: All Ages

Publications and works within these stated levels will, with the permission of Allaah, encompass different beneficial areas and subjects, and will be offered in every permissible form of media and medium. Certainly, the guiding scholar Sheikh Saaleh ibn Fauzaan al-Fauzaan, may Allaah preserve him, has stated,

"Beneficial knowledge is itself divided into two categories. Firstly is that knowledge which is tremendous in its benefit, as it benefits in this world and continues to benefit in the Hereafter. This is religious Sharee'ah knowledge. And second, that which is limited and restricted to matters related to the life of this world, such as learning the processes of manufacturing various goods. This is a category of knowledge related specifically to worldly affairs.

...As for the learning of worldly knowledge, such as knowledge of manufacturing, then it is legislated upon us collectively to learn whatever the Muslims have a need for. Yet, if they do not have a need for this knowledge, then learning it is a neutral matter upon the condition that it does not compete with or displace any areas of Sharee'ah knowledge..."

("Explanations of the Mistakes of Some Writers'", Pages 10-12)

So we strive always to remind ourselves and our brothers of this crucial point also indicated by Sheikh Sadeeq Ibn Hasan al-Qanoojee, may Allaah have mercy upon him, in: *'Abjad al-'Uloom'*,[11]

"...What is intended by knowledge in the mentioned hadeeth is knowledge of the religion and the distinctive Sharee'ah, knowledge of the Noble Book and the pure Sunnah, of which there is no third along with them. But what is not meant in this narration are those invented areas of knowledge, whether they emerged in previous ages or today's world, which the people in these present

---

[11] 'Abjad al-'Uloom', pg. 89

times have devoted themselves to. They have specifically dedicated themselves to them in a manner which prevents them from looking towards those areas of knowledge related to faith, and in a way which has preoccupied them from occupying themselves from what is actually wanted or desired by Allaah, the

Most High, and His Messenger, who is the leader of men and Jinn. Due to this, the knowledge in the Qur'aan has become something abandoned and the sciences of hadeeth have become obscure, while these new areas of knowledge related to manufacturing and production continually emerge from the nations of disbelief and apostasy, and they are called, "sciences", "arts", and "ideal development". This sad state increases every day, indeed from Allaah we came and to Him shall we return....

...Additionally, although the various areas of beneficial knowledge all share some level of value, they all have differing importance and ranks. Among them is that which is to be considered according to its subject, such as medicine, and its subject is the human body. Or such as the sciences of 'tafseer' and its subject is the explanation of the words of Allaah, the Most Exalted and Most High, and the value of these two areas is not in any way unrecognized.

And from among the various areas, there are those areas which are considered according to their objective, such as knowledge of upright character, and its goal is understanding the beneficial merits that an individual can come to possess. And from among them there are those areas which are considered according to the people's need for them, such as 'fiqh' which the need for it is urgent and essential. And from among them there are those areas which are considered according to their apparent strength, such as knowledge of physical sports and exercise, as it is something openly demonstrated.

And from the areas of knowledge are those areas which rise in their position of importance through their combining all these different matters within them, or the majority of them, such as revealed religious knowledge, as its subject is indeed esteemed, its objective one of true merit, and its need is undeniably felt. Likewise one area of knowledge may be considered of superior rank than another in consideration of the results that it brings forth, or the strength of its outward manifestation, or due to the essentialness of its objective. Similarly, the result that an area produces is certainly of higher estimation and significance in appraisal than the outward or apparent significance of some other areas of knowledge.

For that reason, the highest ranking and most valuable area of knowledge is that of knowledge of Allaah the Most Perfect and the Most High, of His angels, and messengers, and all the particulars of these beliefs, as its result is that of eternal and continuing happiness."

We ask Allaah, the most High to bless us with success in contributing to the many efforts of our Muslim brothers and sisters committed to raising themselves as individuals, and the next generation of our children, upon that Islaam which Allaah has perfected and chosen for us, and which He has enabled the guided Muslims to proceed upon in each and every century. We ask him to forgive us, and forgive the Muslim men and the Muslim women, and to guide all the believers to everything He loves and is pleased with. The success is from Allaah, the Most High the Most Exalted, alone and all praise is due to Him.

Abu Sukhailah Khalil Ibn-Abelahyi
Taalib al-Ilm Educational Resources

Publication Translators:

We are presently looking for competent translators in several languages to help translate publications from the English language.

> ## Spanish, French, German, Portuguese, Russian, Turkish, Indonesian, Urdu, Bengali, Russian, & other languages

http://taalib.com/translate

For further information, please visit our affiliate web page here:

http://taalib.com/translate

Online Sales Affiliates:

We now have an affiliate program that enables Muslim around the world to earn affiliate income of any sales they refer to us through the system. With simple sign up, you can download a banner or images and earn permissible income through any sales that coms from your social media account, website. or direct promotional efforts.

> **25%** referred fee for any product order directly referred by you to our sites
>
> **+ additional 5%** retail amount for any order from individual referred by you who also joins the affiliate program

http://taalib.com/earn

For further information, please visit our affiliate web page here:

http://taalib.com/earn

BELIEFS & WORSHIP

30 Days of Guidance [Book 1]: Learning Fundamental Principles of Islaam

A Short Journey Within the Work Al-Ibaanah al-Sughrah With Sheikh 'Abdul-'Azeez Ibn 'Abdullah ar-Raajhee

AUTHOR - COMPILER - TRANSLATOR

Abu Sukhailah Khalil Ibn-Abelahyi

BOOK OVERVIEW

- Interactive course book
- Focused upon both beliefs & principles
- 1st book in 30 Day Series

AVAILABLE LANGUAGES

English

WHO IS THIS BOOK FOR

All age levels

For every Muslim who wishes to live their life in a way pleasing to Allaah it is essential that they ensure that their beliefs and practices actually have evidence and support from within the sources of Islaam. This work approaches this challenge in a way that allows an individual to proceed through discussions related to this a day at a time over thirty days, based upon explanations from one of today's noble scholars.

"...Allaah, the Most Glorified and the Most Exalted, according to a wisdom that is with Him, places those who would oppose the truth in order that the truth be known, and in order that it become something which manifests as something clear and dominant over falsehood."
Sheikh al-'Utheimeen. - Open Door Gatherings 3/66.

WHAT YOU WILL LEARN IN THIS BOOK

Related to essential basic principles of guidance

The role of Islaam in today's world is something which is indisputable and often contested. There are many different understandings of Islaam which range from dangerous extremism, all the way to vulnerable laxity. Yet our well-known scholars continue to work diligently in openly examining and clarifying the false ideas and practices that are attributed to Islaam.

VERSIONS - PRICING

Self-Study Edition (hardcover)	USD $42.50
Self-Study Edition (soft cover)	USD $27.50
Directed Study Edition	USD $25.00
Workbook	USD $12.50
Kindle edition	USD $09.99

PDF PREVIEW

https://ilm4.us/30daybook1

PURCHASE BOOK

http://taalib.com/4134

30 Days of Guidance [Book 2]: Cultivating The Character & Behavior of Islaam

A Short Journey Within The Work Al-Adab Al-Mufrad
With Sheikh Zayd Ibn Muhammad Ibn Haadee al-Madkhalee

> "It is predominant over the other religions and ways of life, as it enjoins the best of deeds, as well as the most excellent aspects of good character, and enjoins the overall well-being of those who worship Allaah."
>
> *Imaam Sa'dee. - "A Summarized Jewel…"*

WHAT YOU WILL LEARN IN THIS BOOK

Related to the subject of perfecting ones character

Some of the questions that this course book helps us answer are: Are you prepared for your reckoning? Are you always working for good while you can? Do you remember the benefit in your difficulties? Is your life balanced as was the lives of the Companions? How do you deal with your own faults and those of others? Do you know what things bring you closer to Jannah?....and more

VERSIONS - PRICING

- *Self-Study Edition (hardcover)*   USD $42.50
- *Self-Study Edition (soft cover)*   USD $27.50
- *Directed Study Edition*   USD $25.00
- *Workbook*   USD $12.50
- *Kindle edition*   USD $09.99

AUTHOR - COMPILER - TRANSLATOR

Abu Sukhailah Khalil Ibn-Abelahyi

BOOK OVERVIEW

- Interactive course book
- Focused upon both character & behavior
- 2nd book in 30 Day Series

AVAILABLE LANGUAGES

English

WHO IS THIS BOOK FOR

All age levels

This course book is intended for the Muslim individual for self-study, as well as for us as Muslim parents in our essential efforts to educate our children within Islaam and our ongoing endeavor of cultivating them upon the extraordinary character and behavior of our beloved Prophet. It is also intended to be an easy to use classroom resource for our Muslim teachers in the every growing numbers of Islamic centers, masjids, and Islamic weekend and full-time schools.

PDF PREVIEW

https://ilm4.us/30daybook2

PURCHASE BOOK

http://taalib.com/4137

30 Days of Guidance [Book 3]: Signposts Towards Rectification & Repentance

A Short Journey through Selected Questions & Answers with Sheikh Muhammad Ibn Saaleh al-'Utheimeen

AUTHOR - COMPILER - TRANSLATOR

Abu Sukhailah Khalil Ibn-Abelahyi

BOOK OVERVIEW

- Interactive course book
- Focused upon both change & growth in Islaam
- 3rd book in 30 Day Series

AVAILABLE LANGUAGES

English

WHO IS THIS BOOK FOR

All age levels

This course book is intended for any Muslim who wishes to improve his life and rectify his heart. Yet this self rectification or purification of the soul must be done in the correct way and upon the correct foundation of knowledge from the Sunnah, if it is to lead to true success in both this life and the next.

Ibn al-Qayyim, may Allaah have mercy upon him, also stated, '*The true purification of the soul and the self is directly connected to those messengers sent to humanity...*"

'The purification of the self or soul and its becoming rectified is dependent upon it being called to account and assessed. There is no purification or rectification nor any possibility of it being brought to a state of well-being except through calling oneself to account.'

Ibn al-Qayyim - Madaarij as-Saalikeen

WHAT YOU WILL LEARN IN THIS BOOK

Related to the Subject of perfecting ones character

This course discusses in detail the inward and outward changes and steps we must take as striving Muslims to improve and bring our lives into a better state after mistakes, sins, slips, and negligence. Discussing real life problems and issues faced by Muslim of all ages and situations -the Sheikh advises and indicates the road to reform, repentance, and true rectification.

VERSIONS - PRICING

- *Self-Study Edition (hardcover)*   USD $42.50
- *Self-Study Edition (soft cover)*   USD $27.50
- *Directed Study Edition*   USD $25.00
- *Workbook*   USD $12.50
- *Kindle edition*   USD $09.99

PDF PREVIEW	PURCHASE BOOK
https://ilm4.us/30daybook3	http://taalib.com/4150

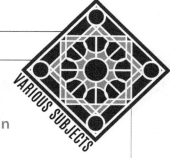

Statements of the Guiding Scholars of Our Age Regarding Books & their Advice to the Beginner Seeker of Knowledge

[Contains A List of over 300 Books Recommended By The Scholars In The Various Sciences Of Islaam]

> "Oh Muslim youth! Oh students of knowledge! Connect yourselves to your scholars, attach yourselves to them, and take knowledge from them. Attach yourselves to the reliable scholars..."
>
> *Sheikh al-Fauzaan. - Explanation of Mistakes, pg. 18*

WHAT YOU WILL LEARN IN THIS BOOK

Sources and subjects of seeking Sharee'ah knowledge
This book is intended to enable any sincere Muslim to strive to proceed with correct methods and manners in seeking of beneficial knowledge for themselves and in order to guide their families. The scholars are the carriers of authentic knowledge and the inheritors of the Messenger of Allaah. Their explantations make clear for us the way to learn and then live Islaam.

VERSIONS - PRICING

- *Hardcover -7.44" x 9.69"*   USD $45.00
- *Soft cover -7.44" x 9.69"*   USD $27.50
- *Kindle edition*   USD $09.99

AUTHOR - COMPILER - TRANSLATOR

Abu Sukhailah Khalil Ibn-Abelahyi

BOOK OVERVIEW

- Taken from words of senior scholars
- Provides road map for Sharee'ah study
- Divided into seven main sections

AVAILABLE LANGUAGES

English

WHO IS THIS BOOK FOR

All age levels
A comprehensive guidebook for the Muslim who wishes to learn about his or her religion with the proper goal and aim, in the proper way, and through the proper books. This question and answer book is for those who seek advice from some of the senior scholars of the current century regarding seeking knowledge, beneficial books, and their warnings against books containing misguidance. Their advice encompasses both modern and classical books in various branches and areas of Sharee'ah knowledge.

PDF PREVIEW

https://ilm4.us/seeker

PURCHASE BOOK

http://taalib.com/79

METHODOLOGY & SECTS

An Educational Course Based Upon Beneficial Answers to Questions On Innovated Methodologies

of Sheikh Saaleh Ibn Fauzaan al-Fauzaan

AUTHOR - COMPILER - TRANSLATOR

Abu Sukhailah Khalil Ibn-Abelahyi

BOOK OVERVIEW

- Interactive course book with 20 lessons
- Focuses upon principles of the straight path
- Discusses modern groups and movements

AVAILABLE LANGUAGES

English

WHO IS THIS BOOK FOR

All age levels

This course book is for any Muslim who wishes to understand the detailed guiding principles of Islaam as discussed by the scholars throughout the centuries, including the scholars of our age. These principles were initially put in place and practiced by the generation of the Companions of the Messenger of Allaah, may Allaah be pleased with all of them, when Islaam was first established, and have been implemented in each and every century by those Muslims following in their noble footsteps.

> "The person upon the Sunnah has mercy. He has mercy on himself through his following of the Sunnah and standing in its shade. This becomes a cause for his success in this world, the life of the grave, and the next life."
>
> *Sheikh Zayd al-Madkhalee - Sharh Adaab al-Mufrad*

WHAT YOU WILL LEARN IN THIS BOOK

Related to the detailed way we understand Islaam

This course focuses upon the importance of clarity in the way you understand and practice Islaam. What is the right way or methodology to do so? Examine the evidences and proofs from the sources texts of the Qur'aan and Sunnah and the statements of many scholars explaining them, that connect you directly to the Islaam of the Messenger of Allaah.

VERSIONS - PRICING

• *Self-Study Edition (hardcover)*	USD $50.00
• *Self-Study Edition (soft cover)*	USD $32.50
• *Directed Study Edition*	USD $30.00
• *Workbook*	USD $12.50
• *Kindle edition*	USD $09.99

PDF PREVIEW   PURCHASE BOOK

http://ilm4.us/minhaj

http://taalib.com/4144

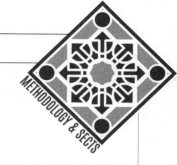

The Belief of Every Muslim & The Methodology of The Saved Sect

Lessons & Benefits From the Two Excellent Works of
Sheikh Muhammad Ibn Jameel Zaynoo

> "Indeed I interacted with the people of the different Islamic groups and organizations, and I've come to see that those that stand upon the call of Salafees are those which hold closely to the Book and the Sunnah as understood by the righteous predecessors of the Muslim Ummah..."
>
> *Sheikh Muhammad Ibn Jameel Zaynoo - "Methodology of..."*

WHAT YOU WILL LEARN IN THIS BOOK

Related to foundation of Islaam & gaining knowledge
This Islamic studies course discusses the different levels of knowledge, important matters related to seeking knowledge, essential study skills, the role of evidence in Islaam, differing and taking from the scholars. Additionally, it explains the central role that the foundation that worshipping Allaah alone should have in our lives, and how that distinguishes every single person.

VERSIONS - PRICING

- *Self-Study Edition (hardcover)*   USD $45.00
- *Self-Study Edition (soft cover)*   USD $30.00
- *Directed Study Edition*   USD $27.50
- *Workbook*   USD $12.50
- *Kindle edition*   USD $09.99

AUTHOR - COMPILER - TRANSLATOR

Abu Sukhailah Khalil Ibn-Abelahyi

BOOK OVERVIEW

- Interactive course book
- Discusses how to study and from whom
- Focuses upon both beliefs & practices

AVAILABLE LANGUAGES

English

WHO IS THIS BOOK FOR

All age levels
This course book is for any Muslim who is looking for an easy-to-follow course- based discussion of not only what it is important to learn but also concise advice on how to study and learn Islaam. Taking selections from two well-known books of Sheikh Zaynoo, may Allaah have mercy upon him, it offers an overview of some of the characteristics and hallmarks which distingushed that clear call our beloved Prophet brought to humanity.

PDF PREVIEW   PURCHASE BOOK

https://ilm4.us/savedsect   http://taalib.com/4141

The Cure, The Explanation, The Clear Affair, & The Brilliantly Distinct Signpost

Book 1: Sources of Islaam & The Way of the Companions-
A Course Upon Commentaries of Usul as-Sunnah' of Imaam Ahmad

AUTHOR - COMPILER - TRANSLATOR

Abu Sukhailah Khalil Ibn-Abelahyi

BOOK OVERVIEW

- Interactive course book with 15 lessons
- Focuses upon sources & principles of Islaam
- First book in continuing series

AVAILABLE LANGUAGES

English

WHO IS THIS BOOK FOR

All age levels

This course book is intended for any Muslim who wishes to connect himself to our beloved Prophet. inwardly and outwardly, in order to walk in his footsteps upon knowledge as a worshiper of Allaah. It is designed to help you, as a Muslim, identify the correct sources, principles, and beliefs of the evidenced methodology of Islaam upon scholarship and proofs, in order to be able to distinguished what opposes them from incorrect sources, principles, and false beliefs.

> "....we know that the beliefs of the righteous first three generations and their methodology is only a single way and path which it is obligatory that we ourselves follow and adhere to. It is that affair, which encompasses within it, that leads to the success of the people." *Sheikh Saaleh Aal-Sheikh, - "Provisions..."*

WHAT YOU WILL LEARN IN THIS BOOK

Related to the independent sources of Sharee'ah guidance

This course book discusses the universal nature and correct beliefs about Islaam as a revealed religion. It also discusses specifically what are the correct evidenced beliefs held by the people of adherence to the Sunnah throughout the centuries about the nature of the Qur'aan, the Sunnah and scholarly Consensus.

VERSIONS - PRICING

- *Self-Study Edition (hardcover)*   USD $50.00
- *Self-Study Edition (soft cover)*   USD $32.50
- *Directed Study Edition*   USD $30.00
- *Workbook*   USD $12.50
- *Kindle edition*   USD $09.99

PDF PREVIEW	PURCHASE BOOK
https://ilm4.us/usulbook1	http://taalib.com/62874

Made in United States
North Haven, CT
23 April 2022

18520079R00052